How To Be A "Better" Human: To Yourself, As An Employee Or A Boss.

Scott M Conrad

Table of Contents

Introduction

Do you feel caught in a rut?

It might be difficult to be trapped in the same location and feel like nothing is changing. When you're languishing, it seems like you're not going ahead toward your objectives. One of the ways to overcome this rut is to take action. Making a deliberate choice to improve oneself may be inspiring and motivating.

But self-improvement occasionally gets a poor name, and for good reason. Our ambition to better ourselves has generated an industry full of terrible hacks that might leave you feeling more frustrated than before, or, that feels wonderful but don't take you ahead.

Working to better yourself may favorably affect your well-being and your connections with family, friends, and coworkers. Let's discuss some things you may attempt that will bring you ahead – become active in your well-being and discover how to work on yourself.

What does it mean to better yourself?
Growth
For some individuals, the concept of bettering oneself is inspiring. For others, it might be more useful to think of it as development. Growth is beneficial and not necessarily a straight line.

Improving oneself is a highly personal path, and the details might alter from person to person. It needs putting in the effort and being ready to suffer pain.

Change is unpleasant. Growth means pushing beyond what you know. But every step you take is part of the journey toward becoming the greatest version of yourself.

Behavior change can be a long process, but it doesn't have to be grueling. Growth occurs by improving simply by 1% every day. Improving yourself may be a series of little habit adjustments, like taking five minutes throughout your day to be more attentive. Or it might be a more comprehensive process, like conquering anxieties.

However, bettering yourself doesn't imply altering the essence of who you are. For example, if you're an introvert, you shouldn't aspire to become an extrovert.

On the other side, if you experience social anxiety, you may practice learning strategies to go through your uneasiness. Eventually, you may entirely overcome your social anxiety so that you may navigate social situations with greater ease.
We are all human, and that means we all have space to develop as individuals, whether it's via our professions or our relationships with the people around us.

Oftentimes, however, we don't know how big of an influence we might have on others or even ourselves.

There are certain minor adjustments you can make in your life today that can lead to tremendous gains in the future and make you not only a better person but also someone who can help others become better people too. Here are some of those adjustments to start implementing today. According to Benjamin Franklin "When you're through evolving, you're finished."

Why is it so vital to learning how to enhance yourself?
There are various reasons to keep working on yourself.

Every time you progress in one element of your life, you might feel more content as you start attaining your objectives. And bettering yourself may aid you in every facet of life.

For instance, bettering yourself at work may help you enhance your job performance, find greater purpose in your career, and even be promoted.

Bettering yourself may also help you enhance your connections, better your capacity to establish boundaries, and build tighter links with the ones you love. Acting to improve yourself is a type of self-care, and if you look after yourself better, you're more likely to have more to contribute to others.

Plus, you may establish growth objectives with your loved ones. Having their support boosts your chances of success, and working together to attain comparable objectives may assist you and bring you closer.

Finally, understanding how to develop yourself is an important quality to have in a world where you must continually adapt. Knowing that you can change might make you more confident about the future and less fearful of discomfort.

You've been there before. You already have a history of effectively developing and improving yourself – you can do it again.

Part 1:

HOW TO BE A BETTER HUMAN TO YOURSELF AND THOSE AROUND YOU

Life may be a tornado of duties and stress, but with the appropriate concentration, you can start becoming a better person and who you want to be. In this book, I'll help you discover how to be a better person in a variety of various ways. From valuing yourself to conducting tiny acts of kindness, there's something you can do each day to develop yourself and grow as a person. It's natural to feel that you might be doing more when it comes to self-improvement. But becoming a better person doesn't mean being unduly harsh on yourself. In reality, it's just the contrary.

The more self-kindness and self-compassion you can develop, the better prepared you'll be to treat people around you the same way.

Plus, doing good for others may give your life a greater sense of significance. It may even assist to enhance your physical and mental wellness.

We've all made errors in our lives that haven't exactly placed us in the greatest light—like bullying someone in school or telling what felt like a small white lie. Chances are, though, you probably felt a little shame and grew because of the scenario.

you'll never be perfect, but that doesn't mean you won't try.

Here's a look at some techniques to weave self-improvement into your daily routine and let go of negative views about yourself and also apply them in your life right away to become your best self.

1. *Make time for rest*

Before you learn how to be great, it's vital to start with the fundamentals. You need to have your fundamental needs satisfied before you go on to self-improvement. Part of it is to make time for relaxation and self-care.

There are many distinct sorts of rest. Are there occasions in your schedule when you have the option to do nothing and take a break? Those calm minutes of repose might help you unwind and evaluate what transpired in your day.

That's why making time for rest may do wonders for your well-being. Plus, when you're well-rested, you'll have more bandwidth to focus on the various ways you may enhance yourself.

2. ***Read more books***
There are books on practically anything. So, reading more books may help you explore your present interests, but also establish new ones. You can even learn a new skill using a book.

Some books are intended expressly to assist you to start working on self-improvement and personal development. You may also read to develop your leadership abilities.

But even being thoroughly interested in a fiction story might do wonders for you. The bottom line is that whatever passions you may have (or be curious about), carve out some time to read about them.

3. *Start a gratitude practice*
One way to learn how to be a better person is by being grateful for what you have.

Practicing gratitude for your current situation can help you avoid feeling bitter about what you don't have.

You don't have to feel grateful for huge things, either. Try to notice the small things that make you happy and make you feel grateful.

You can fine-tune your gratitude practice over time. With practice, it gets easier to naturally think of what you're grateful for. This new perception can change your life for the better. Be grateful for what you have. For so many these days, it's all about what they don't have instead of what they do have. Let's stop trying to outdo each other and instead be grateful for what we've got.

Gratitude begins in our hearts and then dovetails into behavior. It almost always makes you willing to be of service, which is where the joy resides. It means that you are willing to stop being such a jerk. When you are conscious of everything that has been provided to you, in your lifetime and the previous few days, it is hard not to feel humbled and delighted to give back.

You've undoubtedly heard it a million times, but maintaining a gratitude notebook of things you're grateful for may have a major influence on your outlook. Research has shown that adding appreciation into your everyday life may help fend off stress, enhance sleep, and build more pleasant social interactions.

Use the acronym **GIFTS** to help you pinpoint things you're thankful for.
When thinking about things you're thankful for, seek examples of:

Gift: personal growth, such as mastering a new skill.
Inspiration: experiences or things that influenced you.
Friends/family: individuals that improve your life.
Tranquility: the tiny, in-between moments, such as savoring a cup of coffee or a good book.
Surprise: the unexpected or a great favor.
When listing things you're thankful for, be sure to include a mention of why that item makes you grateful.
Write in a journal

Journaling is a terrific technique to enhance your meditation and gratitude practices. It also makes a terrific new hobby.

You may write down the things you're thankful for in your diary. You may also practice how to become more conscious of your ideas.

Plus, evidence suggests that writing may boost your well-being and lessen mental anguish. The same study showed that individuals have strengthened their resilience following the first two months of continual journaling.

When you start writing in your diary, try your best not to censor yourself. Write what comes to mind, and don't judge what comes out.

Practicing appreciation every day might help you be more optimistic. Gratitude is more than a sentiment; it's an intentional discipline. Being grateful and appreciative of your life, no matter where you are in it, helps you be compassionate and caring towards yourself and others. Take a time to understand that kindness may be beyond oneself and that every smile or modest courtesy is a gift.

Here are some additional ways you may nurture appreciation in your life:

Keep a thankfulness notebook or write a gratitude list to emphasize all the things you're glad for each day, large or little.

Savor surprises by appreciating the thought that was put into them.

Share something you're grateful for with others. For instance, if your brother helped you move your furniture, let him know how much you appreciate his aid.

According to a study, folks who maintain gratitude notebooks are more positive and feel better about their life. Additionally, individuals who speak thankfulness are less resentful of affluent people, are more eager to assist others and may avert health risks like coronary artery disease

4. Learn a new language

It's never too late to learn a new language. Learning how to speak another language helps you think differently and perceive everything around you from a new perspective. It may also open up doors for you.

You'll get to immerse yourself in another culture as you study how another language functions differently from English. Plus, you may go to areas where people speak the language you're studying.

Learning a second language may do more than assist you on your trips abroad. It may even benefit you with your professional chances.

More and more firms in most Countries are seeking multilingual talent. Currently, statistics suggest that US firms are struggling to locate enough staff who speak languages other than English.

56% of companies state that their demands for foreign languages in the workplace have risen during the previous five years. And 1/3 of businesses now don't satisfy those demands with their existing staff.

Some of the languages that are high in demand are Spanish, Chinese, and French.

Use the acronym **GIFTS** to help you pinpoint things you're thankful for.
When thinking about things you're thankful for, seek examples of:

Growth: personal growth, such as mastering a new skill
Inspiration: experiences or things that influenced you
Friends/family: individuals that improve your life
Tranquility: the tiny, in-between moments, such as savoring a cup of coffee or a good book
Surprise: the unexpected or a great favor

When listing things you're thankful for, be sure to include a mention of why that item makes you grateful.

Write in a journal

Journaling is a terrific technique to enhance your meditation and gratitude practices. It also makes a terrific new hobby.

You may write down the things you're thankful for in your diary. You may also practice how to become more conscious of your ideas.

Plus, evidence suggests that writing may boost your well-being and lessen mental anguish. The same study showed that individuals have strengthened their resilience following the first two months of continual journaling.

When you start writing in your diary, try your best not to censor yourself. Write what comes to mind, and don't judge what comes out.

Practicing appreciation every day might help you be more optimistic. Gratitude is more than a sentiment; it's an intentional discipline. Being grateful and appreciative of your life, no matter where you are in it, helps you be compassionate and caring towards yourself and others. Take a time to understand that kindness may be beyond oneself and that every smile or modest courtesy is a gift.

Here are some additional ways you may nurture appreciation in your life:

Keep a thankfulness notebook or write a gratitude list to emphasize all the things you're glad for each day, large or little.

Savor surprises by appreciating the thought that was put into them.

Share something you're grateful for with others. For instance, if your brother helped you move your furniture, let him know how much you appreciate his aid.

According to a study, folks who maintain gratitude notebooks are more positive and feel better about their life. Additionally, individuals who speak thankfulness are less resentful of affluent people, are more eager to assist others and may avert health risks like coronary artery disease

5. *Meditate*

Meditation offers you a terrific technique to slow down in a fast-paced environment. Even just a few minutes a day of meditation may help you better yourself and enhance your mental health.
New research has demonstrated that meditation helps lower anxiety, sadness, and pain ratings, particularly during times of crisis.

You'll also become more conscious of your cognitive habits. This attention implies you may learn more about yourself over time. It might help you recognize harmful behaviors that are exerting a negative influence on your mood and your life.

Meditation may also help you practice mindful breathing and increase your self-awareness.

6. Nourish yourself with healthful meals

It's simpler to live your best life when you feel enthusiastic and well-fueled. What you eat has a major effect on how you feel.

Start monitoring what you put in your body. Eat a range of different meals in varied colors throughout all dietary categories.

Try to consume fresh meals whenever you can. If you don't have time to make nutritious meals at home, check for other choices, such as meal kit subscriptions or healthy catering services. Eat at least one meal attentively

When you're caught up during a stressful day, it's easy to speed through your meal without listening to your body.

Mindful eating provides you an opportunity to check in with both your bodily sensations and your emotions.

Pick a meal, even if it's only a sandwich, and take your time eating it. Notice the distinct flavors and textures. It's a form of brief meditation that may function as a simple stress reliever

7. Add extra exercise to your life.
While diet plays a significant factor in how you feel, mobility and exercise also have a role to play.

There's a range of strategies to start moving more. For instance, you may start a new sport and even have a buddy join you to spend quality time with them.

If you're not interested in starting up a sport or joining a gym, you may still find alternative ways to incorporate movement into your life. For example, you may start taking daily walks.

You may also start an exercise regimen from the convenience of your own home. Many free fitness routines are accessible online, which means there's always something fresh for you to do if you grow bored.

If you work in an office (and even if you work remotely), chances are you don't get to spend a lot of time outdoors during the day.

Find chances in your schedule to spend more time outside. If you have access to places of nature, consider spending time there.

A recent study shows that even a short 15-minute walk in the forest can decrease negative moods like anxiety, fatigue, anger, and depression. In the study, forest walks were more effective than city walks.

They were also more effective in participants who had higher anxiety levels.

With the right clothing, you can take advantage of the outdoors even when the weather isn't perfect. Consider saving some money to invest in robust outdoor clothing that can protect you in any weather.

If you take up an outdoor activity, make sure you're well-equipped for it. For example, make sure you have good hiking shoes if you begin hiking.

8. Practice kindness toward others.

Kindness is one of the best ways to become a better you.

First, it's free. It doesn't require much effort to be kind instead of indifferent or unkind.

Second, it can help you feel much better about yourself.

Third, it can improve other people's lives as well. Showing compassion requires you to become more aware of others around you. By doing so, you'll notice more of what others need, even when they don't For example, you may notice a work colleague is suffering with something you can assist with. Or you may notice a stranger fighting to open a door with a baby stroller. This should be clear, yet there are so many people out there who seem to forget how much of a difference compassion can make. When individuals are nice to one other, it's infectious. Compassion fosters kindness, and there's nothing wrong with it. I feel it takes more energy to be nasty, so why bother?

Everybody in our world has their concerns. If we all tossed our issues in a pile and saw everyone else's, we'd grab ours back, isn't that the truth? Caring for and assisting others should be a fundamental human trait. When you notice somebody in need, ask what you can do to assist. Donate to organizations when you can, even if it's a few dollars. We need to be a more caring culture. Practice random acts of kindness Being helpful to others might help give you a feeling of purpose and make you feel less alienated.

Try doing something pleasant for someone at random:

- Pay a compliment to a stranger.
- Buy lunch for your coworker.
- Send a card to a buddy.
- Contribute to someone in need.

You'll notice your mood elevate a bit when you do good for the pure delight of it. Studies suggest that merely noting acts of kindness for one week may enhance happiness and appreciation

Make it a goal to perform one random act of kindness every day. If you've begun journaling, write how it made you feel and how the other person responded.

9. Develop a list of objectives.

If you want to enhance yourself over time, it's vital to start creating objectives.

When you put down precise objectives, you can start monitoring your progress over time. This is another subject you may journal about.

For example, you may establish a goal to walk every day for 30 minutes by the end of the year. You may build up to your objective progressively.

For instance, if you presently take no walks, you may start with short 10-minute walks three times a week. Every week, you may increase the duration of your walks.

And every few weeks, you may add a new stroll to your plan until you accomplish your daily walking target.

10. Work to improve your fear of failing.

Fear of failing might hinder you from taking moves forward to attain your objectives and work on your self-development.

To develop yourself, it's crucial to discover methods to undertake tough tasks, even when fear is holding you back. That's why it's necessary to work on your fear of failing and ease out of your comfort zone.

To improve this phobia, you might start with minor things and work your way up to greater ones. This means you don't have to start by mastering your fear of public speaking by signing up to conduct a lecture at work.

Instead, you may build up to it in modest increments.

For example, practice public speaking in a private situation to individuals close to you whom you trust, including your family or spouse.

Over time, you might start practicing in front of more and more people. Every time you speak in front of someone new, you'll show yourself that you can transcend your fear of failure.

Remember that failure will still happen, and that's alright. Resist the impulse to beat yourself up when you fail. Embrace the setback and consider it as a vital stepping stone in reaching your objectives.

11. *Limit activities that exhaust you.*
Are you realizing that spending too much time looking through social media is sapping away your good mood?
Have you discovered that spending too much time with negative individuals nibbles away at your energy?

Try to identify what satisfies you and what drains you during the day. Some tasks that exhaust you may be inevitable, like revising your budget or food shopping.
But there are other aspects that you have considerably greater influence over.

For example, consider removing social media applications on your phone if you find yourself in a foul mood after too much scrolling. Or attempt to restrict how much time you spend with folks who are continually negative around you.

12. Practice saying no to express your limits

It might be simple to say yes to everyone and everything, even when you don't feel comfortable. This may be true at work and in your personal life.

Some family members welcome you to their house the day you set aside for you-time. You're entitled to say no and keep that day to yourself.

Your boss wants you to have a look at something while you're on vacation. You may also opt to say no.

13. Inner work

Inner work arises when you investigate your inner experiences.

It includes all of the procedures, values, and mental models that you use to navigate the environment. *Some examples include decision-making, spiritual well-being, and self-awareness.*

Inner work may be even more powerful when you combine it with assistance from a coach and a trusted inner group who can help you reflect and take action.

One of the finest ways to develop and improve is to have help. Get someone who can help you see yourself more clearly and who is there to assist you to achieve. You deserve to have someone in your corner.

14. Compliment Yourself

Every morning before you move on with your routine, spend a few minutes offering yourself praise. Whether you complement your wardrobe, hairdo, or how you just performed a job utilizing your particular skill sets, giving yourself a small emotional boost can make you happy. And, when you're content with yourself, that mood may be infectious to people around you.

15. Don't Make Excuses

Blaming your spouse, employer, or customers is unproductive and won't get you very far. Instead of pointing fingers and making excuses about why you aren't happy or successful in your personal or professional life, acknowledge your faults and learn from them. When you do this, you will become a better person. When I began living up to my faults and downfalls, my life turned itself around. I grew happier and healthier, and my relationships improved.

16. Let Go of Anger

Letting go of anger is easier said than done. While rage is a completely acceptable feeling, you can't let it persist. When this occurs, you may make foolish judgments, and more significantly, it may impact your health. Research says bottled-up rage might cause stomach difficulties, trouble sleeping, and possibly heart disease. It's suggested you write your sentiments down, pray or meditate, or learn to moderate your thoughts.

17. *Practice Forgiveness*

This could be the hardest item on this list. I battled with forgiveness for years, as so many other people do. But an Anne Lamott statement eventually persuaded me that forgiving my drunken father was better than the alternative:

Forgiveness means it eventually becomes unimportant that you lash back. You're done. It doesn't always indicate that you want to eat lunch with the individual. If you keep striking back, you remain imprisoned in the nightmare. Holding on to regret, sadness, and hatred not only affects others, but it also harms you. When you experience any of these emotions, it influences your attitude and how you treat everyone, including yourself.

Harboring unforgiveness breeds bad ideas.

Decide to let things go and establish a goal to never go to bed angry

Forgiving isn't about making the other person feel better; it's about making you feel better.

If for no other reason than for yourself, forgive to untether yourself from the terrible experiences of the past. Take time to contemplate, and express gratitude for the insight and understanding obtained through your pain.

Forgiving yourself and others may help you enhance relationships. On your road to becoming a better person, it's crucial to let go of whatever grudges you're holding. The past is in the past; it's time to move ahead. Allow yourself time to forgive your previous errors and realize what they've taught you. Then, forgive those who have wounded you. You may not be able to forget what they've done, and that's good, but forgiving may offer you peace of mind.

Dwelling on past wrongs may raise your blood pressure and pulse rate, whereas forgiveness can assist manage and lessen stress.

Humans make mistakes—even when it's you who makes the error. And sometimes those errors truly hurt. However, instead of dedicating your energy to lingering on that error or feeling terrible, forgive that individual—or yourself—and concentrate on the future. Remember, vengeance isn't good for your health, and the greatest revenge is your success and happiness.

18. Be Yourself.

These include being able to connect yourself with your values and beliefs, define your identity, build bravery, set limits, and discover focus and purpose. Stay True to Who You Are

Be proud of who you are and don't allow anybody else to convince you differently. If you want to achieve greatness, never sacrifice your ideals or integrity for another person. These attributes go hand in hand, you can't genuinely be great if you're not yourself.

The easiest approach to being a better person is to just be 100% you! You are unique, exceptional, and one-of-a-kind. Accepting yourself for who you genuinely are may make you feel happy, enhance your life, and establish your identity. Follow your intuition, do what you love, and explore your interests. The more you do feed your energy, the happier and more confident you'll be.

Enroll in courses that pique your interest to acquire a new skill or discover a new passion.

Do tasks that are significant to you to help you feel satisfied.

19. Know Yourself

The greatest way to tell whether you have all your ducks in a row is to spend some time thinking about what it is that makes you tick. What are your fundamental values? What do you want out of life? How can you attain those goals?

The answers to these questions will assist and guide every single choice you make. Even better, understanding yourself can help equip and empower others since they'll see a mirror of themselves in you.

It's not your position, or what you have, or even who you are or what you have achieved that makes leadership, it is the goal of your innermost passion, the yearning of your heart.

20. Take Risks.

Risks are excellent. The absence of risks indicates you're playing it safe and avoiding venturing out of your comfort zone. There are few things more vital than knowing how to take chances in life. When you confront fear, conquer hurdles, and learn from failure, you become a stronger person for it.

Without these crucial experiences, your abilities as an entrepreneur won't increase very rapidly, and living on autopilot isn't something we should want to accomplish. Accepting risk is crucial to growth as a human and as an entrepreneur.

21. Face Challenges.

We live in an age of self-service when we can order meals via a phone app and have them brought to our front door by someone else. In many respects, we've gotten more isolated. The globe has become smaller owing to developments in transportation and communication, but technology has also left us feeling more alone.

That's why one of the most essential things you can do for yourself is to get out and meet new people and push yourself physically. Challenge your intellect by tackling new difficulties, whether that's taking on new tasks at work or asking someone to dance (no matter how uncomfortable you feel).

When we step out of our comfort zone, it encourages us to be creative and reminds us just how competent we are when pushed.

Take chances and push yourself to attempt new things, but remember that sometimes failure is simply another step on your route to success. Always concentrate on what brings out your best self and makes you feel joyful and alive. Everyone deserves that sensation.

Don't take life too seriously and never forget to laugh at yourself since sometimes failure is simply another term for learning. Just make sure you don't forget to learn from it!

Although it may feel like there's nothing you can do to aid in your present position, there is hope. Apply these basic steps and begin to discover how to become a better human being and allow for improvements inside yourself to take place.

After all, what's healthy for your mental health can only make your physical health better as well. With love, we can all be nicer people and that alone is enough incentive to strive toward being one of those better persons today.

22. Think Positively

Negative thinking may be just as infectious as a cold, therefore it's crucial to keep your ideas positive at all times. Humans are subject to what's called social contagion.

This implies our emotions and behavioral patterns are readily impacted by individuals around us, whether it's at work or on the sidewalk. If you find yourself having difficulties keeping cheerful, consider surrounding yourself with good individuals who will impact you positively.

Use positive self-talk

It's easy to get caught up in being unduly harsh and judgmental of your perceived faults. This negative, unhelpful self-talk might diminish our total drive.

If you're continually telling yourself you aren't a decent person, for example, it's hard to find the motivation to take measures toward self-improvement.

Practice positive self-talk by presenting a fact and following up with some positivity.

FACTS + OPTIMISM = POSITIVITY

The next time you find yourself feeling inept or overwhelmed, try reminding yourself:

"I know this transition is going to be tough, but I've put a lot of important thinking into it and have evaluated all the alternatives given to me [fact], so I feel certain I am doing the best I can in this time [optimism]."

The hard part is catching oneself in the process of negative thinking and consciously opting to think otherwise, but with a little practice, this will become simpler.

23. *Think About What you Want in Life.*

Before you can determine how to live, you need to know what that looks like. Sit down and think about what your perfect existence might look like – what events would be most gratifying for you? What function do relationships play in your ideal life? Work? Health?

There are no right or wrong answers here, but be sure to evaluate everything. Think about all areas of life, not just one component (health) or even just one set of priorities (job). Even if your list changes over time as priorities alter and your life changes, it's a good idea to spend some time pondering what makes up the ideal life for you.

If we don't change, we don't grow. If we don't grow, we aren't alive.

24. Have Fun!

If you're not having fun in your life, it's quite hard to be happy. So make sure that you're doing things that you enjoy, or at least give them a try. That way, even if they aren't what you want to do for a job, at least there will be one pleasant thing in your life.

I suppose most individuals don't fully like their professions because they've never discovered something else that truly fascinates them. Take some time and find out what makes you happy and go for it.

25. Be Open to Change.

Whether trying a new restaurant, going to an unfamiliar corner of the globe, or doing something that has always worried you, you should constantly be open to change. This permits you to develop when you encounter something new. It helps you be high functioning and self-confident if you are not frightened of change.

Positive, achievable ambitions may offer you something to thrive for. Everyone needs something to live for, so think about what you want in life. Not only can aiming for anything make you a happier and better person, but it may also help you discover your purpose. Use a pen and paper and write down the short and long-term objectives you would want to attain. Try asking yourself these questions to determine and define a realistic goal:

Is there a relationship in your life you wish to improve?

What causes or movements are you enthusiastic about?

Is there a project you've been meaning to finish?

What do you prefer to do in your leisure time?

Making your aim to "be a better" person may be tough to define and attain. Instead, go for little objectives that will help you develop as an individual, like reading a nonfiction book, writing a short story, contacting your mom every weekend, or helping someone in need every day

26. Educate Yourself.

If you don't understand why one nation is invading another, take the time to educate yourself on the current situation. Ask a person personally associated with the incident for his or her opinions. Remember, we're all interrelated, and being aware of diverse cultures, different individuals, and what their lives are like may make you a more well-rounded person. This will also help you grasp points of view distinct from your own.

27. Try a digital detox

Unplugging for even a tiny period may be good for your well-being. The next time you find yourself with nothing to do, walk away from your phone for a few hours, consider going for a stroll and connecting with your ideas.

Step away from your phone either for a few hours or perhaps spend the full day off of electronics, consider stepping outdoors and interacting with nature, or meeting up with friends physically. Remember: Even a brief vacation from your phone might help you relax and concentrate on what gives you pleasure.

28. Get adequate sleep

Not feeling properly rested might make you feel cranky and unproductive during the day. Try to obtain seven to eight hours of sleep each night.

Find strategies to increase the quality of your sleep by lowering your caffeine intake late in the day, taking a melatonin supplement, or relaxing in a warm bath or shower before night.

29. Breathe consciously.

Take a minute at the bus stop, in line at the grocery store, or before dozing off to sleep to concentrate on your breathing. Practicing simply a few minutes a day of deep breathing has been demonstrated to activate our body's relaxation response and control stress.

DEEP BREATHING 101

Inhale as you usually would.

Exhale, making sure you take longer than you did to inhale.

Repeat this method until you start to feel calm. If you like to count, try breathing in for the count of 4, holding for the count of 7, and expelling for the count of 8.

30. Clean for 30 minutes

The way you feel about your house might determine whether your time there is restorative or stressful.

The next time you have a free 30 minutes, set a timer and undertake some fast home activities that'll bring a little brightness to your day, such as:

cleaning your bathroom mirrors, hanging that painting you adore but haven't gotten around to displaying, clearing out your desk
Reward yourself by spending some time to appreciate your restored space — make a face mask in your freshly clean bathroom, for example

31. Engage in self-care.
We frequently think of self-care as manicures and spa treatments (which are all fantastic methods to destress). But everyday self-care goes much beyond pampering. It's also about eating healthily and receiving enough nutrients to sustain your brain and body.

Similarly, make sure you're exercising or deliberately moving your body, taking time to interact with people, and having some relaxation or downtime for yourself.

These don't need to be time-consuming tasks. Look for brief 10- or 20-minute pockets of time in your day when you may stroll outdoors for a walk or serve yourself a bowl of fresh fruit.

32. Be gentle to yourself

Many of us have the propensity of dwelling on something that was spoken to us, rehearsing it again in our thoughts. Instead of taking things personally and being self-critical, it's best to express empathy and compassion to the other person, as well as ourselves. Before learning to love others, you must learn to love yourself. Self-compassion may seem like the reverse of becoming a better person, yet caring for yourself is the first step to progress. After all, if you can't care for yourself, how can you care for others? Try these activities to help you be compassionate to yourself:

Pretend you're writing a letter to a buddy in a similar position. How would you talk them through it?

Place your palm over your heart and murmur positive affirmations to yourself when you're depressed, including "I am safe," "I am nice to myself," and "I am clever and have a huge heart."

Note your successes and achievements without judgment by reacting sensibly to self-critical ideas.

Acknowledge where the critique comes from and then show it incorrectly in a reasonable manner.

Look in the mirror every morning and commend yourself. You may remark something like, "You're lovely, no matter what," or "You have the brightest grin."

TIP:
Follow the golden rule "treat people the way you want to be treated" to be a compassionate person.

Think of all the ways you have a good effect on others around you and try writing them down each day. Again, these don't have to be grand gestures.

Maybe you held the door open for someone carrying some heavy bags. Or started brewing a fresh pot of coffee at work when you noticed it was getting low.

If you find you're still struggling to change your frame of mind, Tomorrow is a new day, so if you beat yourself up today about something, let yourself off the hook and start fresh tomorrow.

<u>BE YOUR OWN BEST FRIEND</u>

Try to treat yourself the same way you would a loved one. Would you constantly talk down to your best friend if they had an "off" day and dropped the ball on something?

Hopefully not. And you shouldn't talk to yourself that way, either.

33. *Acknowledge your shortcomings*.
Everyone has defects, but you may seek to improve yours. Notice how your conduct and attitude affect others. Are people typically happy or unhappy around you? Do friends come to you for support or advice? Answering these questions and evaluating your interactions might help you find and improve your limitations.

For instance, if friends don't frequently come to you for guidance, ask yourself why. Do you speak over them or criticize their decisions? Maybe you need to focus on being a better listener.

The more you learn to be flexible and adaptive with your conduct, the more you can care for yourself and the people around you.

34. Control your Anger.

Feeling furious is normal, but too much anger might hamper compassion. When you want to be a better person, it's crucial to grasp the whys and hows of someone else's circumstance. Things may not turn out the way they're meant to, but that's alright. Take a deep breath and realize that you may not be able to control many things, but you can control your attitude.

Try channeling your anger away from yourself and others by going on a walk, performing yoga, or striking a pillow.

Calm yourself down by taking deep belly breaths and remembering a peaceful or pleasurable memory.

Reconstruct your thinking habits by avoiding phrases like "never" or "always" to describe yourself or others.

35. *Be patient*.

Things don't always go the way you'd want them to, and that's alright! Rather than becoming frustrated when things don't go your way, take a deep breath and remember to have patience. It's fine if life is slower. Try relishing these leisurely moments by noting the tiny things and recognizing the benefits in the circumstance.

For instance, maybe you ordered a pizza for family game night, but the deliverer is stopped in traffic. Instead of becoming irritated, consider that the additional time waiting for your pizza has given you more opportunities to choose a game. Plus, you'll probably receive a cheap pizza.

Another example may be that your computer begins upgrading the minute you want to work. Rather than becoming irritated, utilize the additional minutes of leisure to play with your dog, take a stroll, or do some cleaning up.

36. Take excellent care of yourself.

Sleep, eating, and exercise may provide you with the energy you need to be great. If you don't give your body the essential nutrients and rest it requires, you won't be able to serve yourself or others. Stick to a regular schedule that's good for you, and observe how your mood changes for the better. When you support your physical health, you support your mental health.

Aim to obtain at least 7 hours of sleep every night to help your mind and body refresh.

Eat food that nurtures your mind and body. Aim to consume complete foods, but don't limit yourself—it's good to have a cookie now and again!

Do a type of exercise you love for at least 30 minutes every day. Maybe that's walking, dancing, hiking, performing yoga, or kickboxing.

Taking care of yourself is one of the finest ways to make yourself a better person. For example, how can you go outdoors and play with your kids when you constantly feel lethargic? How can you be more effective at work while you're exhausted? Not only will you be happier and more productive, but your loved ones and coworkers will also enjoy it.

37. *Accept that change occurs*.
It's alright if your objectives don't remain the same as you mature. The route of self-improvement isn't a straight path—it bends and twists when you least expect it! Because of this, your short-term and long-term objectives may vary as you go. This is perfectly natural and an indication that you're becoming a better person. After all, you wouldn't be adjusting if you didn't want to improve. Change helps us evolve as people. Instead of rejecting change, you should be open to attempting new things, even if they worry you. For example, you may be hesitant about trying that new Thai restaurant in town, yet you could find your new favorite restaurant.

Besides accepting change, you should also push for constructive change.

Try your best not to dwell on the past. Instead, concentrate on the current moment. Change is inevitable, but you can roll with the punches.

38. Think Before You Speak.

Words may carry a lot of weight. Think about the first time your significant other informed you that he or she loved you. How wonderful did it feel? However, words may sometimes be harmful. Have you ever cracked an improper joke or called someone a harsh name? You probably felt very horrible afterward.

Always spend a few additional seconds thinking about the effect of your words before you utter them out loud.

39. Do the Right Thing

As an adult, you should undoubtedly know the difference between right and wrong.

Let's assume you don't pick up your dog after taking it for a stroll. You don't need someone to tell you that you should clean up the mess. You realize that it's your obligation and that it's not fair to leave it there for someone else to step in.

40. Use Your Strengths.
Remember, your abilities and talents are a gift. Don't let them go to waste. If you know how to play the guitar, then share it with others. It will offer delight to you and the people in your life.

41. Address Your Weaknesses.
At the same time, you also need to be conscious of your vulnerabilities. It's another approach that helps us develop as people. Take the time to develop a list of your deficiencies and establish objectives to improve on them.

If you are a hard person to deal with recognize it. Learn to identify and confront your faults and then discover strategies to make them better

The bottom line.
It's common to get caught up in wanting to become the greatest version of yourself. But becoming a better person begins with treating yourself with the same loving care as you do others.

This involves not judging yourself harshly when your fall short of your objectives and offering yourself tolerance and compassion on your bad days.
Keep in mind that there are numerous methods to become a better person, and those presented here are only a few. Find what feels most pleasant and nourishing and strive to incorporate these into your everyday life.

In summary, keep a gratitude notebook to be more optimistic and caring.

- Take care of your mental and physical health to brighten your mood and be happy.
- Find better outlets for anger, like exercising and performing yoga, to divert unpleasant feelings.
- Expose yourself to different experiences to evolve as a person. Comfort zones are excellent, but they may also be stagnant. Every once in a while, shake up your daily routine, try something new, and venture beyond your comfort zone. Trying new activities that make you a bit uncomfortable may extend your horizons and open your eyes to a fresh viewpoint.
- Make a bucket list of activities you can undertake outside of your comfort zone. Then, spend every other weekend ticking one activity off the list.
- Ask friends to accompany you on your trips for twice the pleasure.

- Experiment with a new routine by heading to a different coffee shop for lunch or taking an alternate route to work.
- Don't be scared to challenge yourself. The unattainable might be reachable if you put your best foot forward.

One of the finest methods to enhance yourself is to educate yourself. Knowledge may go a long way, particularly when it comes to comprehending other people's circumstances. Whether you're in school or not, self-educating may help you develop and expand as a person. The more you know, the more perspective you'll get.

Part of life is evolving and becoming a better person—every day. What actions are you working on to better your life?

HOW TO BE A BETTER HUMAN TO OTHERS

1. Be Honest and Direct

How would you feel if a loved one or business colleague lied to you? Chances are you would perceive it as a betrayal of your trust. If you want to be a better person in either your personal or professional life, you should always speak the truth and describe as clearly as possible what you are trying to communicate. Learn to explain your thoughts, emotions, and ideas openly and honestly.

2. Be Helpful

Whether giving up your seat to an old person on the train, supporting a co-worker on a project, or bringing in the groceries when your husband gets back from the shop, being helpful is one of the simplest and most effective ways to practice being a better person. I find that the more I serve people, the better I feel about myself and everyone around me.

3. Listen to Others

Listening to others and giving everyone a voice is one of the finest things you can do. Being a good listener may favorably impact your life.

Sometimes all folks want is someone to give them an ear and listen to what they're saying. Whether it's your kid with some news about school or a buddy whose marriage is disintegrating, when someone seeks you out and wants to speak to you, commit to listening — not just hearing.

4. Act Locally

It may not seem like a huge issue, but supporting a local organization, donating clothing, or shopping from local farmers' markets or businesses are easy ways you can assist your particular community. You may not be able to rescue the world, but you very well may make a difference in your patch of the woods. Get to know and care for your neighborhood.

If you're seeking to make your area better, volunteering is a wonderful way to get engaged and establish a community. Volunteers are 50% more likely than non-volunteers to have established acquaintances in their areas, according to municipal data.

If you're interested in helping not just your area of the globe but yourself as well, volunteer with an organization that deals with youngsters or elders. Volunteering lets you connect on both professional and personal levels while also giving back and it's one of those things that feels exactly as amazing as it sounds.

Helping others doesn't simply help them; it benefits you too! Research suggests that being altruistic (the act of improving someone else's well-being) boosts mood and overall pleasure. So, try volunteering at a local shelter, giving unwanted clothing, or cleaning up rubbish at the park. Even the tiniest gesture may have the largest effect.

Aim to perform at least one act of kindness every day. It doesn't have to be anything huge or time-consuming. Even posting a sticky note on a public toilet mirror stating, "You're lovely inside and out!" may improve someone's day.

When you serve others, you receive a surge of endorphins that make you feel good. This is known as the "helper's high."

5. Always Be Polite.

How much work does it take to say, "Thank you," or to hold the elevator door open for someone? Not much at all. However, these acts of kindness may brighten someone's day. I concluded a few years ago that it doesn't matter whether someone is incredibly nasty, condescending, or worse. The way someone else acts is not going to dictate my conduct.

6. *Focus on Others.*

There's an ancient adage that we tend to receive back in life what we put out there. And although it can seem trite, concentrating on others goes a long way toward helping you become a better human being and making your community, workplace, or family stronger.

The mere act of smiling at somebody will make them feel good; if they smile back, you've just doubled your pleasure. Maybe they won't grin, but they probably won't frown either.

Simply paying attention to someone is enough to brighten his or her day. And if someone asks how you are doing? Tell him or her, honestly.

Imagining what someone is going through might offer you a fresh perspective.

__*Empathy*__ is one of the first stages to becoming a better person since it improves your compassion. Not only can practicing

68

empathy help you be more sympathetic toward other people, but it also helps you create enduring connections and feel less alienated. Being empathetic helps you earn a friend while questioning your viewpoint. Here are some ways you may be more empathic:

- ***Avoid forming assumptions about individuals and leaping to conclusions.***
- ***Imagine yourself in someone else's shoes or position.***
- ***Actively listen to convey interest and make someone feel heard.***

7. Be Respectful

How would you feel if you had just cleaned your house and someone walked in and tracked muck everywhere? You'd probably be a bit angry that they hadn't taken off their shoes. Take this approach and apply it to daily life. For example, don't drop your garbage or cigarette butts on the floor of public toilets or walkways merely because someone else will pick them up. Be respectful of others' time, opinions, ideas, lifestyles, emotions, work, and everything else. You don't have to agree with any of it, but individuals have a right to have ideas and yours is not always accurate.

8. Don't Show Up Empty-handed

Going to a party this weekend at your friend's apartment? Make sure you don't come empty-handed. Even if you've been promised that there will be plenty of food and drink, bring along a small bit to say you appreciate being invited.

9. Surprise People

How amazing does it feel to make someone smile? It feels wonderful, right? Surprise your loved ones or co-workers now and again, with a present, a night out on the town, or by providing support when you know they might use it.

10. Express your emotions politely.
Using "I" sentences may help you carefully explain feelings. Life is full of complicated and perplexing emotions, and with those feelings comes conflict. You may not be able to control every scenario you're in, but you can control your responses. "I" comments may be used in confrontations or emotionally difficult circumstances to convey sentiments without assigning blame. Check out these ways you may transform these sentences into "I" statements:

"You never listen to me anymore," transforms to, "I feel that my worries aren't being heard."

"I dislike when you yell at the kids," changes to, "When you shout at the kids, I feel disturbed because I want the youngsters to feel respected."

"You're constantly anchoring me. It's not fair!" changes to, "I feel like you're constantly grounding me, and that hurts me."

11. *Be a Hero*

That doesn't imply that you have to put on a pair of tights and a cape. It involves assisting an elderly neighbor with groceries. Opening doors for others. Buying a cup of coffee for the lady in front of you when her card is refused. Listening to a buddy after his relationship recently ended.

12. *Pay Attention to Others*

Doesn't it feel amazing when someone asks how your day went? Try to do the same for others. Even if you have to scribble down reminders in your calendar, it may make all the difference in the world to someone when you follow up with them on significant occasions.

13. *Stop Being Wasteful*

Just because you may have five plates of food at an all-you-can-eat buffet doesn't imply that you have to—waste is a concern for the food service sector. You may also cut water use by taking shorter showers and produce less waste by recycling. And, don't forget that disconnecting equipment while not in use might conserve power. Your part, no matter how minor it may appear, may be incredibly vital for the environment.

14. Greet everyone you encounter

Whether you nod or smile to strangers passing by or say "good morning" to everyone who enters the office, make an effort to acknowledge those around you when you see them, In doing so, you'll notice you might find yourself feeling more present and connected to those around you, even if you don't have a close relationship with them.

15. Don't Be Impatient

When we are impatient, we get angry and may do something we'll regret. Ask yourself, how would you feel if you screamed at your kid or a coworker because you were in a hurry to get out the door in the morning or complete a project? By exercising patience you'll not only make better judgments, but you'll also feel better about yourself every day.

16. Stop Pointing Fingers

When you point one finger, three fingers are pointing back to you. We all confront problems in life, but you can't use them as an excuse to hold you back or to develop as a person.

Remember, you and you alone are responsible for preserving your energy. Give up blaming, moaning, and excuse making, and keep taking action in the pursuit of your goals—however ordinary or high they may be.

Becoming a better person doesn't happen quickly, but it is attainable. Believe in yourself and believe that it is achievable!

PART 2

HOW TO BE A BETTER PERSON IN YOUR JOB

AS AN EMPLOYEE

Human experience goes a long way toward making individuals feel more secure in their positions.

Both papers give good guidance. Yet, the idea that we need to be reminded that we're human and the immense influence mankind has at work is both illuminating and mind-blowing. How in the world did we come to a situation where mankind needed a reminder? Why does the art of being human have to be so complicated? Yet, here we are.

This isn't a history lecture on how we lost sight of the human aspect in the workplace and need to bring it back. Nor is it a sale to companies on why we all need to acknowledge and allow for the human aspect to shine out of every person. Both are vitally significant, by the way.

Today, we're going down the essentials. This is a letter to all of us people out there. Those of us working in an office, striving to thrive in our jobs, trying to make a difference, and prospering (or withering away) is dependent on our connections at work.

While the human experience at work is multifaceted, each one of us may concentrate on our modest acts to notice the humanity in others around us, and so bring out our own.
There isn't just one secret to success in work. There are numerous aspects of effective employee talents. It all starts with

the effort that you're prepared to devote and your tendency to develop excellent connections with your colleagues. It's crucial to be purposeful when you immerse into your profession. Reflect on your personal and professional objectives and be sure to obtain input from your colleagues and your supervisor. If you treat each day as a chance to make a difference, you'll discover pleasure and success.

1. Be a Team Player

One of the most essential behavior objectives for workers is to function as a cohesive team. The American Psychological Association addresses the influence of collective objectives on behavior and the performance of workers. If your objective is to be one of the most valuable workers in the business, you can't achieve it alone. Strive to cooperate effectively with others and demonstrate the conduct that is beneficial to cooperation

If being the new person at work feels daunting, try your best to reach out and become part of the team. Demonstrating a true desire in learning, combined with helping out others, can make you feel comfortable and part of the group. Teamwork offers other rewards, too. You're more likely to feel more dedicated to the company and be more productive if you participate in cooperation. The silver lining is that you'll have an enhanced chance to create new connections and engage with colleagues.

2. Work on Your Communication Skills

Strong communication skills are fundamental to success in work. It's vital to be clear and timely when you interact with people. If you work hard to let people know what you're doing and when you'll get it done, your colleagues will know that they can rely upon you. Communication skills can also help you communicate with people when you're feeling tension or disagreement.

Do your best to enhance your cross-cultural communication abilities. Becoming culturally competent can help you connect with all of your colleagues and be an integral member of the team.

3. Avoid Gossip and Negativity

Don't get misled into chatting about your colleagues. If you participate in unpleasant discourse, you're likely to be viewed as a troublemaker, rather than a productive member of the team. Instead, concentrate on keeping a good attitude and persuading people to be loyal to the team. Your boss will appreciate your goal to be a better person in the office if you keep focused on work, instead of rumors about others.

4. Go Beyond What Is Expected

Work hard and demonstrate that you want to be the employee that your manager can depend on. One of the hallmarks of an excellent employee skill set is an employee who doesn't settle for the bare minimum. Stretch yourself to look beyond your standard job description. Develop a solid connection with your supervisor and explore how you may effectively contribute to the objectives of the business. Your ambition and initiative will set you apart from others.

5. Seek Feedback and Advice

It's vital to ask your supervisor for input on your performance. Don't wait until a scheduled review session to discover how she feels about your work. If you consistently inquire about how you can improve, you'll know where you stand. Additionally, you'll convey a message to your manager that you want to be a distinctive employee. Be careful to take her/his words of advice and apply them to particular performance objectives for growth.

If being the new person at work is frightening, try contacting an experienced employee to serve as a mentor. Some organizations have official mentorship programs, but if not, it's appropriate to take a manager or respected employee to lunch and ask for their ideas. Networking and creating contacts with the best and the brightest will position you to learn about what it takes to be successful in the company.

6. Establish yourself as a dynamic employee by creating personal objectives for self-improvement. Consider a list of activities in the workplace that are characteristic of an excellent employee. If you engage in self-reflection, you can determine what you need to do to stand out among others. As you move toward demonstrating excellence, ask for feedback from your supervisor and colleagues. Knowing how others see you will help you have a full understanding of what you can do to make a difference.

7. Be a Go-Getter

A sense of direction is imperative if you are going to understand how to contribute to the organization. Beyond the tasks that need to be accomplished, personal goals can jumpstart your career trajectory and empower you to work hard.

8. Stay Motivated

Have you ever felt bored at work? One of the advantages of setting a personal goal is that you will feel more bonded to the work at hand. You're also more likely to work hard and feel positive about your role in the organization.

9. Stay Connected

When you set goals and share them with your supervisor, you're more likely to connect your interests to the organizational mission. Your role will feel even more meaningful when you see how your goals contribute to the desired result of the team.

10. Remain On Track

Be sure that your goals have tangible timelines for completion. Create a method to push yourself to chip away at the tasks connected to each goal. Don't wait until the day before the deadline to get your work done.

11. Demonstrate Your Worth

If you create quantifiable objectives, you'll display everything that you do to contribute to the team. Weave into the mix how you contribute to a pleasant work environment and what you do to tackle times of conflict to showcase your positive conduct in the workplace.

12. Stay for the Long Haul

Setting and accomplishing objectives can help you stay interested and employed.

You're more likely to continue with an organization if you feel like you are helping and can measure your work with transformational aims.

13. Avoid Gossiping

The work environment is full of diverse characters. You will inevitably work with someone who rubs you the wrong way or is intimidated by your success. Resist the urge to disparage others. If you become a gossiper, you're likely to end up on the wrong side of teamwork.

14. Be Kind

Go out of your way to show compassion for others. Most managers consider kindness as the No. 1 priority on the list of behaviors in the workplace. If you're considered someone who invests in the success of others, you will rise to the top. You never know when you might end up supervising your colleagues. Demonstrating compassion can make you

feel better about your actions and guarantee
that you are valued by others.

15. Collaborate and Cooperate

Often, the workplace is a competitive
environment. You may be seduced into
keeping ideas from others for fear that they
would exploit them to advance their
self-interests. Instead of operating in a silo,
aim to cooperate wherever feasible.
Employees that work hard to collaborate
with others are crucial to a synergistic team
environment.

16. Follow the Rules

Workplace regulations and guidelines are
examples of behavioral objectives for
workers. Managers have a lot of things to
worry about and, first and foremost, they
are seeking workers that don't offer an issue.
If you are conscious of the regulations, you
won't be branded as a demanding employee.

17. Timeliness is Key

It may sound like a no-brainer, but you may be astonished at the number of workers who cheat the clock. Time theft is a tough problem to tackle. Ask yourself whether you have ever done any of the following:

- *Added time to your timesheet*
- *Punched in early*
- *Punched in for someone else*
- *Took extra time for lunch or a break*
- *Did personal things on corporate time*

Even if you believe the boss will never know, one of your co-workers will notice. Force yourself to remain committed to corporate regulations and procedures and it will pay you in the long term.

18. Stay on Top of Tasks

Don't procrastinate. When you're given a deadline for a job, get it done on time. If your boss can trust you for deliverables, you will be considered a reliable employee. Tackle the less-desirable duties first and you'll be astonished at how much simpler it is to get through the day.

19. Be Honest and Ethical

Have you ever strolled out of the office with a working pen or "borrowed" a stapler for personal use? Have you ever watched a coworker lie to their supervisor? A Survey data released in the Harvard Business Review found that 23 percent of workers feel compelled to act unethically. If you see anything, say something. You may start by talking to the employee involved, but don't let it go if they aren't receptive. Even if you're terrified of being called a snitch, acting ethically is one of the most critical behavior objectives for workers.

20. Push Yourself to Communicate.

Improving your communication skills should be at the top of the list of behavior goals for employees. Interacting effectively with a wide variety of constituent groups will enable you to do your work at a high level.

21. Over Communicate.

There isn't a way that you can communicate too much. It's easy to stay in your work cocoon, but you need to connect with others to get the job done. Here are some things that you can do to improve your communication skills:

Listen, Listen, Listen, and Challenge yourself to listen more than you talk. If you find yourself speaking first in most situations, back off and let someone else take the lead in a conversation.

Be Inquisitive.

Rather than dominating the debate with your thoughts, seek input from others before contributing your two cents.

Conflict Resolution

Most individuals shy away from confrontation. The concept of addressing someone is often unpleasant and intimidating. If you tackle conflict resolution with an attitude of care and relationship-building, the result is typically beneficial. If you feel under-resourced to be a conflict-resolver, put this as one of your instances of behavioral objectives. Seek training and professional development to strengthen your talents.

Ask for Feedback

It's crucial to know how you are seen as a communicator. Regularly question your boss and coworkers about what you can do to enhance your relationship-building abilities. If feasible, do a 360-profile exam that involves your colleagues in reflection on your communication abilities. You may think that you're a great communicator, but how do others feel about your style? Work hard to address your weak places so that you may serve as a role model for others

22. Embrace confrontation (the healthy sort).

We're all different. Surprise! Well, not a surprise. We all "know" we have various opinions and perceptions. We simply have a hard time recognizing that fact. What if we were able to notice such differences, be inquisitive about understanding them, then have a talk about those differences with an open mind, no judgment, and a desire to explore different routes forward? Sound utopian? It may be. But if we're able to develop individual skills to handle differences in opinion, it is possible — sometimes. Even just a modest improvement could lead to a breakthrough, or simply more respect for the fellow human sitting beside you.

23. Be dependable.

If you say you'll do something, do it. There are a few ways to break trust faster and easier than not following this basic credo. When you are reliable, people turn to you.

They are open with what they need and they know they can count on you. In turn, they reciprocate, and when you ask for what you need, ta-da! You have a gaggle of humans willing and ready to help you get where you want to go.

24. Compete.

I don't mean to compete in the cutthroat, dog-eat-dog sort of way we've come to expect in corporate environments. I mean it as a driver for success. You can be more and accomplish more, but you need a good motivator to get you going. It's different for everyone, and once found, it can propel individuals, teams, and organizations to succeed at levels they couldn't imagine. This is the power of humanity. And it starts with a desire to achieve – not at the cost of others, but alongside the humans around us. Tap into that fundamental drive and see where it leads.

25. *Get out of your comfort zone.*
Complacency is death. Sure, feeling comfortable can be satisfying, but it's also limiting. Stepping into something new, while scary, is also enthralling. It has power and possibility. Instead of allowing yourself to do the same mundane tasks, day in and day out, pick a new project. Commit to tackling a challenge. Take a class. Write a speech and give it. Show your vulnerability and reap the rewards. Not only will you impress yourself, but you'll inspire another human. And that's an invaluable return.

26. *Have fun.*
Seriously, have fun. Make it a mandate. If your coworker is stressed, down, frustrated or all of the above, make it your mission to lift his spirits. Share a story of your misery that ended in success (or failure, as long as you overcome it eventually!). That saying "misery loves company" may feel good at the moment, but that person who made you laugh or smile, even when you thought it

wasn't possible – that person stays with you forever. At the end of the day, isn't that what life is about? Enjoying the good and the bad with the humans we interact with?

No doubt, this isn't rocket science. It's just not happening. At least not at the scale it could. Imagine the impact if each of the 230 million knowledge workers in the world were to consistently focus on these simple actions. The power would be astounding.
Now it's your turn. Take a moment and ask yourself, "Am I consistently doing these things, day in and day out?" If the answer is no, I implore you to get out there.

Be human! Your co-workers are waiting for you.

AS AN EMPLOYER (BOSS)

As a leader, you are continually flooded with new procedures, management styles, and ideas to help get more out of your staff. You could easily develop a library of the leadership and management books that have been produced in the last decade alone. Human relations skills are not a procedure or technique; they are an attitude to work and life

Maintaining excellent interactions between managers and workers is crucial to the success of any company or organization. Strong employee relations may produce better job satisfaction, more productive workers, and a strong community in the company. Learning how to build and maintain strong employee relations will help you establish a healthy work environment that maintains and attracts top talent

Whether you are an employer in your firm or you are promoted as a manager in a specific organization, it's always a good thing to keep studying how to be a better boss. If marketing helps a firm boost its sales, human resource management, on the other hand, helps it assure effective and efficient production. Here are some ways to be a better Boss to your subordinates:

1. *Begin with praise and honest gratitude.*

The most significant word in this statement is "honest". Honesty is one of the most vital attributes of a leader. Your comments hold weight as a leader, thus you must be honest in your praise. The best method to be honest in your gratitude is to have a really specific example to back up your praise and admiration. It will also assist reinforce the desired activity and result in the future. As a leader, it is crucial to be believable. Sincere and effective communication in the workplace is crucial. You want to be sure that you are not doling out fake praise.

People will see straight through flattery and your words won't carry the weight they require for you to lead successfully

2. Call attention to people's errors all indirectly.

In today's "gotcha" culture when individuals are quick to bring out a mistake or a defect, it is easy to become defensive or for workers to shut off. By bringing attention to a person's error indirectly you take some of the stings out of the interaction. Everyone makes errors. A successful leader utilizes human relations skills to deal with the error beneficially so that it may become a learning experience rather than simply a painful exchange

3. Talk about your faults before blaming the other person.

Another technique to cushion the shock of a mistake is to bring up your faults. Not only does it highlight the adage that "no one is perfect", but it may also be a chance to show

how you learned from the error and were able to grow. That being said, there will always be some dumb blunders when nothing can be done other than life through the repercussions and move.

4. Ask questions instead of providing plain direction.

By posing a question you allow your staff to fill in the spaces on their own. You will seldom have to answer a question and the employee never will throw back the burden of the choice to you, which is extremely typical in the manager-employee relationship

5. Let the other person save face.

This is one of several key management and leadership abilities. When errors or obstacles arise, it is natural for an employee to take it very personally, particularly if they are involved and genuinely care about the task. By helping someone save face you provide your employee the option to safely recover from a mistake

6. *Praise the least progress and every improvement.*

Be "hearty in your approval and effusive in your praise". As a leader, whenever you witness an activity that you wish to encourage, you should always express particular appreciation. It is human nature to crave favorable comments. Additionally, when you are coaching an employee, praise may operate as a light to direct people toward the final objective

7. *Give the other individual a wonderful reputation to live up to.*

This talent is a bit of anticipatory praise to encourage the action that you want to see as a manager. However, when you practice this idea openly, be sure that you are not setting up a person to fail with a task or work that could be too enormous

8. Use encouragement.

Make the mistake straightforward to rectify. When correcting faults, another interpersonal communication method is to assist unravel the issue. Even the best workers make errors. Mistakes may decrease confidence and participation. As a leader, it is crucial to assist staff to shake off errors and move on constructively. By cultivating these leadership skills, you will learn to give encouragement and a rapid solution that may enable someone who might be down swiftly recovered from a mistake

9. Make the other person enthusiastic about performing the item you recommend.

Out of all of the human relations abilities that might make you a better boss this one is the least specific. As a leader, you need to know your staff. By understanding your personnel, you can discover angles to get them interested in various initiatives. Why speak about what we want? That is childish. Absurd. Of course, you are interested in what you desire. You are perpetually fascinated by it. But no one else is. The rest of us are exactly like you: we are interested in what we want.

10. Create an open communication.

Asking your staff for suggestions about ways the business might improve frequently leads to innovative ideas that benefit the whole workplace. Establishing a conversation between you and your team not only delivers vital knowledge, but also tells your team you respect their perspective. When your team members provide recommendations for improvement, appreciate their comments to demonstrate you respect their thoughts. Try implementing some of the suggestions team members give. They may act more inspired to work toward a goal if they helped construct the steps to get there.

11. *Communicate the company's objective and vision.*

Help workers understand how their work fits into a wider organizational structure and how their positions connect to the company's strategic goal. Sharing the company's basic principles may produce more meaningful experiences for team members. Communicate changes in expectations, rules, and procedures in both written and conversational forms to appeal to a wide variety of communication types. Consider sending emails or organizing team meetings to alert staff of changes. Employees generally enjoy openness from employers, so supply your staff with adequate information to build a more productive environment.

12. *Make staff feel appreciated*

Expressing thankfulness and praise for a job well done may dramatically boost an employee's attitude toward the business and make employees feel valued. Finding diverse methods to convey thanks makes workers feel appreciated. Encourage positive reinforcement by noting when workers accomplish something, even if it's something minor.

Public acknowledgment encourages some personality types. This form of acknowledgment also demonstrates to other workers the kind of work ethic they may strive toward. Try creating an Employee of the Month award to publicly acknowledge one great employee and create an incentive for others to try to surpass this accomplishment. Consider different approaches to reward accomplishment in the workplace for personalities who prefer less public recognition.

13. *Promote work-life balance.*

Employees typically view work-life balance as a crucial part of the workplace and search for companies that do the same. Creating a work environment that offers workers the freedom to pursue hobbies outside of the workplace may eventually develop a stronger workforce and encourage better interactions between employees and management. Options like paid time off, the option to work from home, health benefits, and flexible work schedules contribute to a good work-life balance in a firm.

Work-life balance goes beyond organizational regulations. Managers having compassion for the challenges their workers endure outside of work may make a difference in not just that employee's well-being, but their general perception of the organization. You may foster strong employee relations by demonstrating support when workers need time for personal leave. Do not overwork your personnel. Their lives do not simply revolve around your business - they also have families with whom they must spend quality time.

14. Offer professional development opportunities

Employees having the ability to learn and grow in their professions via professional development opportunities frequently feel happier and more productive at work. When workers understand the career path for their role, they may create clear objectives and discover what abilities can help them get a promotion. When feasible, ask workers about what sorts of skills and experiences they want to learn and change their responsibilities or job requirements to assist them to reach their working goals. Consider giving tuition reimbursement for career development-related educational programs to assist workers to grow toward their overall objectives.

Starting a mentorship program that connects junior employees with experienced professionals within the company is another way to build employee networks and help team members feel more fulfilled at work. Mentors can guide entry-level employees to develop actionable plans for achieving career goals. They can also offer advice when their mentees experience a challenge in the workplace.

15. Fulfill your promises.

Your employer-employee relationship should be based on trust. Hence, be true to your words and fulfill your promises if you want your employees to trust you. Did you promise them a company beach outing? Deliver it and don't break their hearts.

16. Be transparent.

You don't need to hide your company's problems from your employees. If you trust your workers, you have to let them know your organizational problems and ask for their help. They are a part of it anyway, aren't they? Asking your employees what they can help with shows that you have faith in them. It boosts their worth and motivates them to work harder.

17. Spend quality time with them.

In any relationship, time is essential to keeping it healthy. Grow your employer-employee relationship by spending quality time with them. Do personal coaching, have lunch with them, treat them to dinner, and engage in other fruitful activities that will strengthen your connections with them.

18. Respect them.

Your staff or workers are not just laborers, but they are also your company's important resources. Without them, your business will have less or even zero production, and without production, it will not generate revenues and profits. Thus, treat them with respect, honor, dignity, and pride. Never treat them as your company's expense, but as your company's valuable assets.

19. Be a role model.

A great leader was once a great follower. If you want to be a better boss or manager, show your employees how to get things done. If you want them to achieve their targets, achieve your targets. If you'd like them to always clean their workspace, always clean your desk. If you wish them to always be on time, be on time always. In other words, lead by example.

20. Be a better listener.

It's usual for bosses to be good speakers, but it's rare for them to be good listeners. Be an extraordinary boss by giving your employees the privilege to speak and be heard. This will enhance their communication skills and improve their self-confidence. This will also improve your knowledge, awareness, and understanding of your team members, helping you to formulate better management decisions in your organization.

21. *Appreciate your employees*.

Don't be a credit grabber but give the credits which are due to them. Give your workers the reward they deserve for a job well done. Although they are getting paid for their time and work, there are still priceless things that you cannot compensate for with money. These unseen things include their trust, loyalty, and faith in you.

22. *Be accountable.*

Don't be a blame-thrower. As the boss or the head of your company or department, you should realize that you have the greatest responsibility. You can hold an employee responsible or accountable for the mistakes she or he commits, but you should not forget to take your share of the blame or liability.

23. *Encourage physical health*.

Let them take a power nap. Let them enjoy their lunch and coffee breaks. Conduct regular sports and fitness activities. Encouraging a healthy body, mind, and lifestyle benefits not only your employees but also your company's productivity.

24. *Be generous*.

If you like your workers to give their best or work for more than what you are paying them, then be generous. Generosity begets generosity. So don't be too stingy. Do not underpay your employees but rather pay them for more than what they deserve, especially if your business is already thriving. Give bonuses and gifts so they will also gift you extra time, care, and effort to grow your business.

25. *Encourage discipline*.

Too much kindness will not make you a better boss. It will only give birth to abusive and undisciplined employees. Without discipline, there is no progress. That is why you should set rules and policies in your company, and strictly implement them. Don't hesitate to give punishments and penalties to your employees if they deserve them. Remember that a great leader doesn't only have a soft heart but also has tough hands.

26. Challenge them.

Don't let your employees get bored with unchallenging and routine tasks. Instead, teach them how to go out of their comfort zone and push their limits. This will help them achieve professional and personal maturity. Give them challenging tasks, and trust them.

27. Share your vision.

To inspire and encourage your staff, offer them direction. Show them your destination. Tell them about your company's goal and vision. Make them feel like they are a part of your company's ambitions and aspirations.

28. Be practical.

Learn how to choose your fights. A prudent leader will not go into a conflict that she or he cannot win. Likewise, a good manager should not also create objectives or targets that are unreasonable. If you give services to customers, don't make promises that your team cannot fulfill. It will only put your staff and your company in peril.

29. Show positive feelings.

A simple grin or friendly welcome might immediately brighten up their day and motivate them to work harder. Of course, you can only achieve this if you can learn the ability to keep yourself cool in any sort of scenario.

30. Encourage self-discovery.

Buy personal development or self-help books for your staff. Let them attend leadership and motivational workshops. Provide them paid vacation time for exploring and finding their true self.

31. Encourage independence.

Train your staff on how to make choices on their own. Teach them how to have initiative. This will not only let them experience autonomy, but it will also enable you to outsource other decision-making chores to save time and let you concentrate on other vital concerns in your business.

32. Show that you care.

Make your workplace pleasant and safe for your staff. When they are unwell, visit them. When they have family or personal troubles, ask if you can assist them. A superior manager is also a hero to her or his workforce.

33. Train yourself.

Learning and training are not just for your workers, but they are important for supervisors and managers. Don't stop acquiring new management and leadership abilities. Read new books or undergo courses that can help you strengthen your leadership abilities further.

All of these elements are closely connected to enhanced human relations abilities and interpersonal communication in the workplace. They are simple, yet each, if done really and sincerely, may drastically increase your leadership abilities and effectiveness. Look around at the top leaders in your company or the business community, you will notice each day how they demonstrate these important leadership traits and human relations abilities to get the most out of their team.

RESULTS OF BEING A BETTER EMPLOYER.

Employee relations describe an organization's endeavor to develop good connections between team members and their employer or management. Human resources experts often aid in employee relations by recognizing and addressing difficulties at work, monitoring and increasing employee morale, and offering assistance to the company's management. In smaller organizations, managers often execute these activities.

1. Improved communication

Strong employee relations may increase communication across all aspects of a firm. Having an open avenue for workers to submit feedback helps their feeling of well-being and contentment. Effective communication between employers and workers also makes it simpler for management to hear ideas for ways to enhance their leadership style and practices.

2. Enhanced motivation

Employees having a favorable relationship with the company's leadership generally feel more motivated at work. Motivated individuals might exhibit an initiative to finish duties and a drive to surpass expectations to achieve achievements. Use employee feedback to discover what inspires workers. Consider utilizing employee ideas to steer rewards, gratitude, and recognition inside your firm.

3. More employee buy-in

Buy-in refers to an employee's adherence to business principles. Improved employee relations may lead to higher buy-in from team members working toward corporate projects and goals. Building good connections between management and workers improve engagement and move a business toward completing objectives as a team.

Employees are more likely to succeed when they know that their function influences the overall performance of the firm. Improved employee relations may assist team members to grasp the company's goal and their position in attaining it, which can make employees feel like they are a part of something greater than themselves. Creating a feeling of community in the workplace may help create connections among team members which can lead to higher pleasure at work.

How can you build a better workplace?

Maintaining a good work environment helps enhance employee morale, retention, and productivity. Here's how to enhance your workplace.

Boosting your office's work environment involves offering workers room and privacy to complete their job, making the workplace more pleasant, and improving communication.

Hosting business events and showing thanks creates trust and generates excitement.

To help keep productivity and morale strong, don't underpay staff or expect them to work through their breaks.

Your work environment affects your emotions, drive, mental health, and performance. If employees work in a drab workplace atmosphere with unpleasant personnel, they generally won't have the confidence or job satisfaction to speak out. That's why having a good work atmosphere is crucial to your company's success. We'll discuss how to develop a healthier work environment that keeps people happy and motivated.

Creating a better workplace generally needs common sense, subtlety, and sensitivity.

Seeing your staff as persons instead than business instruments is crucial.

Here are some strategies to enhance your work environment, and employee engagement in turn.

1. Hire exceptional team members — and don't be afraid to let ineffective ones leave.

Successful organizations recognize that a pleasant work environment begins with employing workers that suit your culture. Ensure your staff is professional and team players. This also goes for folks already on your team. Employees who work with toxic individuals are more likely to become toxic themselves, plunging your firm into an unfavorable work environment.

Tip: When terminating an employee who's been dragging down your team, ensure you've given them adequate criticism and opportunity to change. If termination is unavoidable, concentrate on the facts and make sure you have sufficient paperwork.

2. *Improve the lighting in your workspace.*

Lighting has a critical impact on workers' performance and attitude. A 2021 analysis by academics verified old awareness that exposure to natural light might increase mood, vitality, and mental health.

If it's not feasible to include natural sunlight via windows, there are alternative options:

Blue-enriched light bulbs. Blue-enriched light bulbs may decrease tiredness and boost happiness and job effectiveness. Use this style of lighting in brainstorming areas.

Warmer-tone bulbs. In conference or break rooms, employ warmer tones to induce serenity and relaxation.

Middle-tone bulbs. In meeting rooms, employ moderate tones that welcome workers while keeping them awake.

3. Make the workplace comfy.

A tidy, pleasant workplace may have a huge influence on the relationships between co-workers and management.

Even if the sun can't shine into your office, make an effort to establish a soothing ambiance with nice furniture, working equipment, and a few extra-mile comforts.

For example, allow your staff the freedom to work where they're comfortable. You may furnish the workplace with comfy seats and offer them an option of whether to sit or stand at their workstations.

Make it easier for [employees] to acquire items like exercise balls and plants on the corporate dime

When workers pick a setting that makes them comfortable, allow them the opportunity to modify their area, since everyone works differently, do away with the "same-issued everything" and give everyone a budget to create their setup.

Open-format workplaces attempt to increase communication and cooperation. However, open-office etiquette, such as respecting privacy and valuing organization, is vital to this setup's success.

4. Improve communication with staff.

Be cautious of how you engage with staff. Team members and higher management should concentrate on their communication strategies – including inclusive communication efforts – and their influence on building a healthy work environment.

Employees are driven and feel appreciated when they're given positive feedback and shown how their work contributes to the success of the firm. This includes designing employee performance goals and delivering detailed feedback on how their job contributes to the organization's larger reach.

But workers shouldn't be the only ones being assessed. Managers should be receptive to comments as well.

When you include your team in decision-making in an attempt to create a better work environment, they feel appreciated. Don't be scared to ask workers for their input on a new perk given or what they think of a new client project.

5. *Host business events to boost involvement.*

Hosting company-wide events help boost employee engagement. The more workers socialize, the more they form ties with one another and their bosses. Attending business events may make workers feel like they're a part of a work culture that appreciates more than finishing projects on time. It may provide kids with a feeling of belonging combined with an opportunity to exhibit their identities.

The morale boost that commonly accompanies these engaging activities may offer workers extra optimism to bring with them each day at work. You may organize a corporate lunch, a treasure hunt, a day at the fair, or an hour at an escape room.

6. Express thanks to your team.
While you're focusing on communication, don't forget to demonstrate thanks for your team's hard work, effective employee recognition may alter and elevate a business.

It generates passion, boosts creativity, fosters trust, and delivers bottom-line outcomes. Even a simple 'thank you when an employee goes above and above on a project, or puts in a series of late nights, goes a long way.

Why is a pleasant work environment important?

Creating a healthy work environment encourages and engages your staff, leading to increased job satisfaction and employee retention within your firm. Your workers will feel less workplace stress and be more eager to contribute suggestions for your company's success to assist your business development and prospering.

A healthy workplace environment may enhance productivity, cut absenteeism, and, in some sectors, reduce workers' compensation and medical claims.

To assist establish a stress-free work environment, consider creating a staff health and wellness strategy to decrease weariness, sickness, and burnout.

What does a poisonous workplace atmosphere look like?

A toxic work environment has several telltale signs:

- A lack of proper communication among employees
- Managers who communicate unclear or incorrect information
- An adverse work-life balance among team members
- Employees who take very little time off
- Disrespectful employees and managers

Company culture is perhaps the most obvious toxic office environment indicator. When a company prioritizes business outcomes at the expense of employee retention, job satisfaction, and mental health, the office environment will be toxic.

What does a good work environment include?

A good work environment values corporate success and employee satisfaction equally. If you concentrate on building a pleasant work environment, ensuring your company's culture encourages a healthy work-life balance. Some methods to achieve this include:

1. ***Allow remote work.***

Developing a telecommuting policy that enables your staff to work from home sometimes or full-time may enhance their work-life balance and contribute to a healthy work environment. In 2022, A Research Center surveyed over 5,800 workers in the U.S. to analyze how the COVID-19 epidemic altered work arrangements. Among responders who now work a few days remotely out of the week, 64% feel their work-life balance has improved.

2.

2. *Implement flexible work policies*.
Flexible work practices include hybrid, compressed, and diversified work schedules that work best for individual workers. Flexible scheduling may enhance employees' work-life balance and raise their productivity.

3. *Practice open communication.*
To further develop a healthy work atmosphere, allow an unrestricted flow of ideas among workers and management with no fear of harsh criticism.

4. *Add meaningful employee perks.*
Positive work environments frequently feature extensive employee benefits packages with fair regulations for vacation and paid time off as well as mental health days.

5. *Encouraging employees to seek professional development* which may produce engaged individuals interested in defining and following a career path and contributing back to the organization.

What aspects should you consider while developing a pleasant work environment?

When developing a healthy work atmosphere, consider your actual office area. Ask the following questions:

- *Do your staff have adequate room to accomplish their task without invading someone else's space?*
- *Are you offering your workers appropriate privacy while ensuring they stay honest about how they utilize their time on the job?*
- *Are you giving locations where employees may take breaks or discuss work concerns with their co-workers?*

You also must think beyond your office space and consider other elements. Ask the following questions:

- *What opportunities do you provide for fun team-building group activities that can increase morale and help achieve your company mission?*
- *Are your employees clear on your company's mission?*
- *Do you permit remote work when employees feel sick or must take care of personal needs at home?*
- *How many vacations, personal, sick, and paid days off do you allow?*
- *What are some work environment mistakes?*

Avoid the following common mistakes while you're creating a positive work environment.

- *Don't ask staff to work through breaks. No matter how hectic work can become, avoid asking staff to continue through lunch or other breaks. Overworking personnel might raise their stress. Without breaks, workers won't be able to withdraw and clear their brains. Breaks could seem unproductive in the short term, but in the long run, breaks can enhance productivity.*

- *Don't neglect learning chances. Instead of merely pointing out an employee's mistake, explain how they may prevent repeating it. Gently help them comprehend how to improve, and be open to give aid whenever required. This technique may make your staff feel more comfortable approaching you for support.*

- *Don't ignore employees' interests. Disregarding your employees' passions might make them feel that there's no space for uniqueness and expression on the job. Instead, find methods to integrate your employees' hobbies into their job. A 2021 study indicated that the COVID-19 epidemic left 56% of workers eager to give more to society. Merging work and hobbies might provide workers with a stronger feeling of worth as they could be more involved in their job. For example, let's imagine an employee has exhibited a talent for editing videos. In such a situation, you may discover a method for them to contribute to the company's future marketing campaign or video live stream.*

- ***Don't underpay personnel. Underpaying employees can have detrimental effects on the workplace environment. Aside from increased employee turnover and a negative brand reputation, underpaying employees can quickly lead to a hostile workplace culture. It can also lead to more stress and poorer attitudes among employees. To help your employees feel valued, pay them what they're worth. Their morale, engagement, and motivation will likely reflect how much they enjoy being appreciated.***

When determining employee salary ranges, consider all forms of payment your employee will receive, including bonuses and allowances.

**Building a healthy atmosphere**

A pleasant work atmosphere may keep individuals present, engaged, and satisfied about their careers. As you attempt to enhance your office environment, keep consistent with the procedures you're establishing. Your workers will likely notice the difference and enjoy the adjustments – and so will you.

HOW TO MANAGE MICROAGGRESSION AS A BOSS

Many pieces of training and literature regarding microaggressions concentrate on how you can intervene in the moment, which is a critical aspect of allyship. But in addition to acting, there are also critical ways to help individuals who encounter microaggressions, structural injustices, and other obstacles to opportunity – and one way is via micro affirmations.

In contrast to microaggressions, micro affirmations are modest ways that you may affirm someone's identity; acknowledge and validate their experience and competence; create confidence; generate trust; encourage belonging, and help someone in their profession. Micro Affirmations may help alleviate and disrupt the detrimental impacts of historical oppression, institutional injustice, cultural marginalization, and personal prejudices.

Here are several to try:

Keep an eye out for critical occasions that could be essential in someone's life, and acknowledge them.

<u>Micro Affirmation#1:</u> Get to know others, and pay attentive attention to their words and thoughts
Show genuine inquiry and care for the lives and work of your team members and coworkers. Build connections with them so

you can better cooperate and advocate for each other. When they are speaking, listen and be present. And while they are expressing their opinions or experiences, make sure you demonstrate compassion and empathy.

<u>Micro Affirmation#2:</u> Mirror the words that someone employs to express their own identity

Listen and discover how someone pronounces their name, expresses their identity, and uses their pronouns. Then echo the phrase they use to describe themselves – it tells them you're paying attention and that you care about them.

<u>Micro Affirmation#3:</u> Acknowledge major religious and cultural festivals and life milestones

Keep an eye out for critical occasions that could be essential in someone's life, and acknowledge them.

Birthdays, births, graduations, promotions, and marriages are all good opportunities for you to send a brief remark. And make sure you check in with harsher lifetimes too, such as deaths and sickness.

A person who is feeling marginalized or excluded, tokenized, or like an imposter may sideline themselves – by not speaking out, not participating, and not turning up.

Micro Affirmation#4: Work hard to promote engagement from everyone on your team
Solicit ideas and comments on projects. If you're conducting a meeting or a project, openly welcome involvement from everyone, and if someone has not contributed, ask them to express their opinions either in the moment or later.

<u>Micro Affirmation#5:</u> When someone isn't engaging, take attention and assist them

A person who is feeling marginalized or excluded, tokenized, or like an imposter may sideline themselves – by not speaking out, not participating, and not turning up. In the remote workplace, individuals may switch off their video because they aren't engaged, don't have a home setting they want to present on video, feel excluded, or are burnt out by injustices and exclusion. Check-in with them, and see if and how you can support them.

<u>Micro Affirmation#6:</u> Acknowledge people's expertise and skill

People with underrepresented identities often find their expertise and skills are regularly questioned and held to higher standards. Make it a point to recognize their experience and talents, and seek their comments and suggestions.

In one study, nearly two-thirds of women in engineering reported having to prove their expertise repeatedly, compared to 35 percent of men — their expertise was questioned, their successes were discounted, and they were often pressured to let men take the lead, while at the same time they were asked to do office housework.

Knowing these prejudices exist, detect when someone's skills and ideas are being questioned and counter that by appreciating their knowledge and providing them chances to shine.
If you've been requested to deliver a speech or presentation, ask if you may bring an experienced colleague with you to the stage.

Micro Affirmation#7: Recognize people's successes.
One of the finest methods to communicate with your colleagues, team members, and the world is by acknowledging their accomplishments. This might be in little

ways, like acknowledging someone's vital contribution to a project in conversation, or bigger ones — such as through public communications or prizes.

Micro Affirmation#8: Amplify their voices

Use your platform to magnify someone else's ideas and stories – this might be via marketing, communications, presentations, reports, verbal storytelling, vendor management and procurement, product and service design, or any other manner that your platform can elevate fresh voices and ideas. Make sure you credit their ideas and voices, boost their stature, and share your impact.

Women — tend to get less quality feedback that might help them make critical course adjustments and grow as leaders.

<u>Micro Affirmation #9:</u> Invite someone to speak and share their skills
If you've been requested to deliver a speech or presentation, ask if you may bring an experienced colleague with you to the stage, or consider stepping back and suggesting someone who isn't regularly asked to speak.

However, as someone who has done this many times, I've discovered that if someone is suffering from imposter syndrome or if they are struggling with a lot in their life, they may say no or not react to your offer. Try again, and let them know why you desire their expertise. And if you're asking someone to contribute their experience at a business event or at an event that produces a profit, make sure they have compensated appropriately for their skill.

<u>Micro Affirmation #10</u>: Provide frequent and excellent formal and informal feedback

Women tend to get less quality feedback that might help them make critical course adjustments and grow as leaders. This might be due to preconceptions or avoidance when supervisors are uncomfortable or scared of how someone might perceive their statements.

When women do receive formal feedback, it is often about their communication styles (for example, you're too aggressive or not assertive enough, or your speaking style can be off-putting) rather than actionable developmental feedback about skills (for example, you could deepen your knowledge about skill X, which will help you in Y way)

<u>Micro Affirmation#11</u>: Establish ahead of time what actions and talents reflect competency and leadership in a job

Tie progress and feedback to team and company objectives, utilize the same feedback criteria for everyone in that job, and establish a plan with each employee to enhance their abilities and manage career growth. Also offer employees valuable comments on presentations, projects, and leadership moments.

Micro Affirmation#12: Provide both positive comments and critical criticism

It's best to offer two to three pieces of specific positive feedback before delivering negative or critical commentary. It may make a tremendous difference in their next performance: You boost their confidence, assist them to understand what works, and then urge them to try something new.

Micro Affirmation #13: Provide subtle feedback in presentations and idea sharing.

Even in a video conference or at a meeting when you're not speaking, your facial expressions and body language may be a valuable source of feedback for others. Make sure you are present while someone is sharing, and think about the message you're expressing nonverbally.

You may not demonstrate your thinking and take in their thoughts, suggest you want to know more, let them know you're baffled by one of their arguments, and so on.

FINAL THOUGHTS

Becoming a better boss requires a lot of patience, dedication, self-control, and even compassion. It also demands ongoing study and practice. You may confront a lot of disappointed expectations as the fact is that people are tough to control. However, as long as you are honest, and you can manage to lead yourself first, you will have a higher opportunity to be a successful boss.

Remember that you cannot boss others if you cannot boss yourself.